AF556733

Steve Parish · Jan Parish

Australian Rainforest

Steve Parish
PUBLISHING

Mist-enveloped rainforest, Wooroonooran National Park, North Queensland

The serpent dreaming in the heart

Aboriginal Australians told
of a Dreamtime serpent,
maker of mountains,
progenitor of rivers,
creator of forests.

Later comers to the southern continent
feared the serpent's children,
coveted the serpent's country,
destroyed forest and forest creatures
with axe and fire.

To some of us, time has bought wisdom.

In the heart of the disappearing forest,
where the serpent dreams
of green beauty recovering the land,
we stand in wonder, sharing the dream.

Above: In the heart of the forest
Opposite: Green Tree-snake

Rainforest australia - A personal discovery

Steve Parish

Above me, the sun flickered and danced in the blue-blackness of impending sunset. Descending, I became entangled in an enveloping forest, whose twisted branches scratched the numb skin of my freezing-cold hands. I sank further, my mind calculating temperature, air available, time since departure. Then, destination reached at last, I stopped and hung in space. I swung around and looked behind me, tilted back and looked above me. The view was overwhelming.

I was in the only forest I had ever known, a forest which had never known the gentle patter of rain. It grew from the rocky sea bottom in sixty metres of ice-cold water, and I peered towards the distant surface through a tangled mass of coral sea fans. I was twenty-two years old and made my living by jumping out of Navy helicopters into the sea as a Search and Rescue Diver. In my spare time, I followed one overwhelming obsession - diving to photograph the sea-creatures found in the deep reefs off Jervis Bay, in southern New South Wales. The sea was my home. During sorties flown over the land, I looked down at rainforest valleys with little interest, never imagining I would ever clamber through their green mysteries.

I was to be just thirty years of age before I entered a rainforest. The year was 1976 and I was now employed by the Queensland National Parks and Wildlife Service. I had been commissioned to go north to the tropical rainforest of the Atherton Tableland, there to photograph the Service's new emblem, the Herbert River Ringtail Possum. My guide was to be Doctor John Winter, possum-expert extraordinary. It was to be my first assignment on dry land, and I was filled with anticipation.

I remember the first night of our quest very clearly. On the eve of my thirtieth birthday, we departed Atherton for the forestry tracks of the Tablelands in an ancient, battered Land Rover bristling with spotlights. Reaching our destination, we drove slowly down dark tunnels of trees. John, sitting on the vehicle roof, held a powerful spotlight at eye-level, "painting" the branches with the beam. If, by good fortune, the light caught a possum, he told me, its eyes would glow as its retinas reflected the light. This sounded to me like a very tall story and I sat in the rear of the vehicle, armed with cameras and flashes, not feeling terribly hopeful. I was soon reassured by our first possum sighting. My guide was a man who could think like a possum and who seemed to know by instinct just where and how high to shine the spotlight to find his prey. Once the animal was frozen in his circle of light, he knew from the colour of the eyeshine just what species he had discovered.

We drove on into the night, John spotting possums as we went. The trees were starkly illuminated, then plunged once more into darkness so deep that I wondered how any possum found its way around in the gloom. As the light glanced across the branches and leaves, I saw resemblances to the deep-sea coral branches with which I was so much more familiar. I had re-discovered my undersea forests on dry land!

That night I photographed a Lemuroid Possum, Long-tailed Pygmy-possum, Green Ringtail Possum, and Common Ringtail Possum. I saw owls, snakes, frogs and geckos, revealed by huge, lamplike eyes, transfixed by the light. I learned from John that little was known of the distribution and behaviour of many of these fascinating rainforest animals.

Opposite: Rainforest palms, North Queensland

After two weeks of magic nights had passed, we had visited a variety of places. Amongst the most remarkable was Mount Lewis, where, above a certain altitude, the spectacular cream Daintree River Ringtail Possum lives in a unique relationship with the vegetation that provides its food and shelter.

I had talked for long hours with people who loved the rainforests and had learned that these magnificent stands of trees, with their stunning floral galleries and remarkable wildlife, were being destroyed daily by clearing. Animals were disappearing.

Back in Brisbane I continued my career as photographer and nature interpreter for the Queensland National Parks and Wildlife Service. I now had a particular interest in rainforest, but over the five years that followed my conversion I discovered that "selling" the idea that rainforests were worth keeping to the general public was not easy. I spent countless nights showing slides, countless hours in contact with the media through promotions and making films, and I came to appreciate that I had lived in an insulated world, my attention focused underwater. I discovered that people had a variety of opinions and emotions about rainforest. Some saw rainforests as threatening, dark places. Some feared being lost in the forest, or being attacked by (imaginary) wild creatures. A few, to my horror, openly expressed support for logging the rainforest. And they would do so while walking through a beautiful stand of trees and showing every evidence of enjoyment.

I found myself with a new obsession replacing my passion for diving. I wanted to make people see the rainforest as the world of wonder it truly is - an "Everyone's Ark", crowded with rare and precious plants and animals.

RAINFOREST shares the experiences my wife and partner Jan and I have had in some of the world's most spectacular rainforests, where we have made far journeys of the mind and spirit without ever having had to leave Australia. From Cape York, Queensland, south through tropical and temperate rainforest to the ancient beech forests of Tasmania, we have encountered unique plants and wildlife and marvelled at the beauty around us.

Australia's rainforests have endured for millions of years, shrinking as the continent has grown ever more arid, until they are making a final desperate stand against the eastern margin. Rainforests are under threat and, unless we act to save them, they will be whittled away. Their remains will eventually be fenced into a few National Parks, where a few living trees will be displayed behind barriers like dinosaur skeletons in a museum.

This book shows the gifts rainforest has given us. We hope it inspires you to share these precious gifts with us and, in return, to join us in giving rainforest the love and protection it needs so desperately.

Below left and right: Daintree River Ringtail Possum and Australian Rhododendron, both found in the Mount Lewis area
Opposite: Mount Lewis, North Queensland

Growing up in the rainforest

Jan Parish

When I was a child, I lived with my family in one of the original cottages built in the Dandenong Ranges, in Victoria. Its beams and stumps were of hand-hewn timber, and its rock chimney was never without a haze of smoke produced by the ever-burning combustion stove. The cottage was between the towns of Sassafras and Kallista, nestled beside a creek deep in a gully filled with giant Mountain Ash and ferns. The sun shone only briefly into this gully each day, its face hidden by tall timber until late morning, disappearing again behind the trees at three in the afternoon. On many winter mornings the frost, and occasionally snow, lay in a light blanket over the green world outside our drafty little cottage.

Growing up in a family of eight children in such a small house meant there was no "room of one's own" and I had to create privacy and solitude for myself. Fortunately, the forest was at my doorstep.

The natural world filled me with curiosity and wonder, for there I could be alone in my own universe of imagination. At every opportunity, I escaped from that little house and the many chores I was expected to perform and disappeared into the gullies. Ducking into the eerie twilight under the tree-fern fronds, I would enter my own world, where I could play out fantasies of fairies, elves and goblins dancing in a tree-ferned forest.

A creek flowed through the gully. Sometimes it gurgled underground, only to reappear triumphantly, bursting up through boulders, creating cascades and little waterfalls. In places, it flowed past sandy beaches, scattered with flecks I thought were gold. In the sand I found smooth brown mussels, favourite food of water rats. Large yabbies, clad in various combinations of red, white and blue, lived in holes in waterworn patches of red clay. When disturbed, they defended their territories fiercely, hissing, with claws stretched upwards.

With my sisters, I walked from Sassafras to Kallista and back on many-stepped, graded paths, crossing bridges over creeks and gullies. Every trip to school was a living nature-study lesson. There was one particular place where the track crossed the road where, on misty mornings, we would sometimes encounter a lyrebird. It was a heart-stopping moment when, peering through the ferns, I would see the male bird dancing, his melodious mimicry echoing through the mist, his lyre-shaped tailfeathers curved over his head.

Below: The Crimson Rosella is common in the Dandenong Ranges
Opposite: Fern forest, Dandenong Ranges, Victoria

I was rather more intimidated by wombats which, because I was small, appeared very big creatures indeed as they lumbered through the forest.

I learned about wallabies on a walk through a paddock of bracken fern taller than I was. As I pushed my way through the lofty stalks, I heard a loud "thump-thump", like a very large person taking two rapid, heavy steps. I was terrified and turned to run, but the unseen monster crashed away. Later, I realised it was a wallaby and was told that the two thumps were an alarm signal.

Night-time was possum-time. Great big brushtail possums were in abundance (and yes, we did think that Yowies lived in our ceiling). I loved the pretty little ringtail possums, they seemed so sweet, though there came a sad day when we began to find them dying, hanging by their tails, which still clung to branches. No-one knew why.

By that time, the Dandenongs had become a popular place to live and to visit. The yabbies had begun to disappear from the creek and marauding cats and dogs had made lyrebirds very scarce. Traffic to our once-secluded area was increasing and wombats and wallabies were now more often seen dead on the roads than alive in the forest.

Even though mist and rain were the most usual weather conditions, still there were marvellous things to see and do. When the great-winged black cockatoos came to visit, wheeling in great flocks through the towering trunks of the Mountain Ash, we would know bad weather was on its way. In winter, flocks of Crimson Rosellas would visit our old walnut tree, decorating the leafless branches in gorgeous reds and blues. One day, a Gang-Gang Cockatoo lighted on a wattle whose seed was just right for a feast. I thought he must be a "king parrot" because of his grand crest. I was enchanted by him and kept a lookout for many years, but he never returned.

There were unbelievable numbers of birds in our forest. Waking before dawn, I would first hear the kookaburras laugh. Then silence. Then the kookaburras would call again, followed by the whole dramatic, splendid dawn-chorus.

No fire had ever burned our rain-fresh gullies between Sassafras and Kallista, but in summertime fire was a frequent threat to the western side of "The Hills". One summer in the 'fifties was particularly bad and even our towns were at risk. As black clouds of smoke filled the skies, families were instructed to evacuate. Down the mountains we drove, to wait in the houses of friends for either bad news or the all-clear.

It was from that year of fires that we noticed the dwindling of our avian orchestra. Many other factors could have contributed. Pesticides and herbicides, no doubt, did enormous harm. Blackberries, whose delicious, finger-staining fruit we loved to pick, had become a pest, and some potent sprays were used to eradicate them, including the infamous defoliant Agent Orange. This would have contributed to the loss of birds and of other small creatures from our forest.

"Development" went on. The once-narrow gravel roads were widened. As I walked to school each day, I watched the earth-moving machines taking huge slices from fern-covered banks, exposing rich chocolate soil and bright red clay. A well-known wombat burrow up on one bank disappeared and the material excavated buried another, lower burrow. I felt terribly angry at the destruction of my beautiful world. Even after the bush healed, it was not the same. We never saw wombats or echidnas again and the rare lyrebird mimicry was now of honking car-horns and crowing roosters.

Opposite: Creek and tree-fern, Dandenong Ranges, Victoria

I learned as much as I could about my forest. At Kallista State School, Mr Hodge, the Headmaster, taught me for three years, as he coped with three grades in one room, poor man. I have always regretted that I never told him how his talks about nature nurtured in me a never-lost curiosity and love of all things wild.

There were other forests, I discovered. I went to Gippsland in the 'fifties and visited the Tara Valley, where I met the true "old" temperate rainforest in small stands in the gullies of the Strzelecki Ranges. Myrtle Beeches are the ancient giants of these forests, which are the last remnants of a green mantle that once covered vast areas of incredibly steep hills. In the eighteen hundreds, land in the ranges was granted to settlers who ravaged the forests with clear-felling and fire to establish dairy-farms.

Unfortunately, rainforest trees do not regenerate after fire and so most of these unique forests were lost forever. The feeling of antiquity in what little is left is awesome, and to me the ancient moss-covered trunks of the giant beech trees create a delicate, intimate feeling. It is dismaying to realise how little there is left of this exquisite creature - I think of it as a creature, because it is a living organism, whose plants and animals are interdependent. Its body can grow, dwindle, or be changed, for example by fire, whose aftermath often sees eucalypt species mingling with rainforest. If no further fires occur, the eucalypts will tower above the canopy for a time, then be overtaken by re-emerging rainforest species.

Childhood and girlhood passed. I moved to Queensland in 1964 and was introduced to Lamington National Park, where I indulged my senses in a world of voracious vines and strangler figs, epiphytes and orchids. Lamington became my haven, where I renewed my physical and spiritual being. Through years that were sometimes difficult for me, the rainforest never failed to sustain me.

Since then, I have discovered other rainforests, with someone who also feels their enchantment, my husband Steve Parish.

We have travelled together through the Daintree and Cape Tribulation forest, which has a lushness and beauty so exotic it is almost decadent. Here, the dark, glossy cut-out leaves of climbing aroids creep up lofty treetrunks and white-flowering ginger perfumes the air. High in the canopy, purple, green and yellow pigeons feed on fruit, and brilliant Ulysses and Cairns Birdwing Butterflies flutter past.

Another of our favourite places is Eungella National Park, which we visited after rain, when mist cocooned mountains and ferns were unfurling new copper and pink fronds. The diversity of ferns and epiphytes was staggering. We were blissfully unaware that not far from where we walked indiscriminate logging was destroying vast areas of this unique ecosystem. We revisited this glorious place recently. There had been crippling drought and it was like visiting a well-loved friend, to find that friend ill and suffering.

Always, rainforest has been to me a place where I feel removed from stress. It is a place where only nature and I exist and in its green depths I can clear my mind and connect with my inner soul. The Dandenong Ranges of my childhood are still there, changed though they may be. I hope that their forests, and all the other rainforests of my life, will continue to exist and to work their enchantments on generations to come.

Opposite: Tarra-Bulga National Park, Gippsland, Victoria, was heavily logged at the turn of the century
Following pages: Russell Falls, Mount Field National Park, Tasmania

From forests primeval

The lifespan of an individual Antarctic Beech tree may be 3000 years, and that is awe-inspiring enough. However, it is even more awesome to realise that the tree's remote ancestors were becoming established as the Age of Dinosaurs was ending. The ancestral beeches were amongst the first flowering plants, and around 60 million years ago, when Australia was still part of the southern supercontinent Gondwana, beech forests were widespread across the continent. Today, these majestic trees remain only in limited areas with temperate climates and copious, reliable rainfall.

Above: Antarctic Beech (Nothofagus moorei), *Lamington National Park, Queensland. This species grows above 600 metres altitude*
Opposite: Myrtle Beech (Nothofagus cunninghamii), *"The Ballroom", Cradle Mountain-Lake Dove National Park, Tasmania*

Life-giving rain

The term "rain forest" has only been used since 1903, when the German botanist A.F.W. Schimper used the word *regenwald* for a community of plants whose almost-touching tree crowns form a closed canopy, allowing only small amounts of light to filter to the ground below.

All closed forests depend upon substantial, regular rainfall. This gift from the heavens cascades upon the forest canopy, patters through palms and epiphytes and drifts in mist-wraiths through the towering treetrunks. It is the lifeblood without which the rainforest and its ecosystems would wither and die.

Above: Rain on tropical rainforest fruit
Left: Raindrops decorate a palmleaf with diamonds
Below: A sun-shower in subtropical rainforest

Inside the waterfall

To gain the inner sanctuary,
slip past the silver scarf of spray
shielding the stern black rock-face.
Once inside, there is safety.
Rest awhile and watch
dim images of the outside world
shimmer on the cascading silver screen.

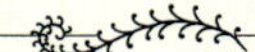

The gift

"Waterfall" *notes the map*
and I trudge the track
expecting water trickling over rocks.
Round a final corner - and through the vines
I see a miracle, a revelation
of spindrift and mist, a bridal veil flung
down over glistening, torrent-silvered stone.

Beneath a blanket of mist

In 1832, the naturalist Charles Darwin wrote of the "sublime grandeur" of the tropical rainforest, and the extraordinary evaporation which took place after rain. "At the height of a hundred feet", he wrote, "the hills were buried in a dense white vapour, which rose like columns of smoke from the most thickly-wooded parts ...".

Three-quarters of the rain falling on a closed forest evaporates, or is transpired by the vegetation. It clothes the forest in mist, rises as vapour, then hangs over the forest as clouds, which shield the canopy from the sun's rays. Eventually, the moist air cools, the water vapour condenses, then falls as rain upon the forest and its surrounds once again.

Above: Morning mist, Lamington National Park, southeastern Queensland
Opposite: Mist clothes the mountain slopes of Eungella National Park, Queensland

Sunlight powers a green machine

Before European settlement, Australia contained perhaps eight million hectares of rainforest. Today, only about two million hectares are left. If all these remaining rainforests could be brought together, they would fit into two circles, one about 70 km in diameter representing mainland forests, another half its size standing for the rainforests of Tasmania.

There are many different sorts of rainforest in Australia. The major types are classified as tropical, or monsoon, or subtropical, or warm temperate, or cool temperate forest. All are leafy factories, whose functions are powered by sunlight.

Above: Moss and tree both require sunlight. Bunya Mountains National Park, Queensland
Opposite: Sunlight filters through palms in Eungella National Park, Queensland

Following pages: Unique and threatened, Fan Palm forest near Cape Tribulation, North Queensland

The successors

Competition is obvious in the rainforest plant community, but so is cooperation. Every tree, standing sometimes precariously in often shallow soil, reaches skywards, so its leaves can spread themselves in the energising rays of the sun. Each basking tree-crown is a flag of victory, held aloft triumphantly by a forest giant. However, each of these trees bears aloft epiphytes, creepers and vines, while around its base grow smaller trees, waiting their turn to stretch upwards and spread their leaves. Viewed from the air, the canopy is a marvellous interlocking jigsaw of leaves of every imaginable shade of green.

Above: Canopy, subtropical rainforest, New South Wales
Left: Tropical rainforest reaching for the sun

Strangle your host and survive

The strangler fig clambers to the canopy on the body of a host tree, which eventually succumbs, bequeathing the fig its place in the sunlight. In 1848, in his *Narrative of a Visit to the Australian Colonies*, the English naturalist Backhouse noted that, after the strangler's bird-dispersed seeds have germinated in a cavity of a host tree:

> "...they send roots down to the ground, which, in their course, adhere to the tree: these again emit transverse, or diagonal, roots, that fix themselves to others in their course downward. Those that reach the ground thicken rapidly, still spreading themselves upon the face of the foster-tree, which, at length, is completely enclosed. These gigantic parasites rear their towering heads above all the other trees...spreading their own roots in the earth, from which also, they sometimes grow without the aid of other trees to sustain them."

Above: Strangler fig on host tree
Right: The strangler fig does not have to compete for canopy space if it can take the place vacated by its dead host

Galleries of fantastic plants

Tasmania's magnificent Gondwanan forests showcase the fascinating Pandani. This giant of all the heaths may reach ten metres in height and, with its pineapple-leaved crown and drooping skirts of defunct leaves, gives a tropical air to the cool temperate rainforest. The lichens which proliferate in all rainforests are stranger still, for each is not one organism but two, co-existing cosily for mutual benefit. A lichen consists of fungal threads which meld together to form "leaves", inside whose tissues shelters one of the blue-green or green algae. The alga utilises photosynthesis to transform raw materials into sugars, which are used by the fungus. The marriage is a happy one, for it has existed almost since plants reached dry land and lichens exist where no other plant life can survive. In the rainforest they play a vital role in humidity control.

Above: Lichen from Tasmanian cool temperate rainforest
Opposite: Pandani (Richea pandanifolia), *"The Ballroom", Cradle Mountain-Lake Dove National Park, Tasmania*

The world of ferns

Ferns are very primitive plants, which have complex sex lives. The familiar fern plant produces asexual spores, which drift on the wind, alight on a favourable spot and germinate into small, easily-overlooked plants called "prothalli". These produce male and female cells. Ferns grow best in damp environments, because the male cells need a film of water in order to swim to the female cells. Once the female cells are fertilised, they divide and become young fern plants, which take root. Then the cycle begins again. Some ferns, such as the brackens, spread by sending out creeping rhizomes, reducing their dependence on moisture.

Above: Beetle on fern frond, North Queensland
Right: Ferns, Lind National Park, Victoria

Ferns their fronds unfurl

The trademark of ferns is the way in which the tips, or croziers, of new shoots unroll, unwinding like springs.

Australia has about 430 species of ferns, nearly three-quarters of them found in rainforests. These ferns grow in a variety of situations. Some are epiphytes, growing on the trunks and branches of trees, while others climb towards the light unaided. Some species cover the ground in great profusion, crowding out other plants. Where there is a break in the forest, ferns spring up to take advantage of the additional light.

Above: Fern unfurling its crozier

Unchanged through ages

Ferns have a fossil history extending back about 350 million years. In Australia they were prominent between 275 and 245 million years ago, growing in dense masses mingled with mosses and horsetails in cold, swampy bogs. Today, their fossil remains are mined as coal. The forms and internal designs of those early ferns have been passed down almost unchanged to their far-distant descendants. A cross-section through the trunk of the tree-fern shown on this page would closely resemble a section made across the petrified trunk of a tree fern which grew some 255 million years ago, with a main stem containing water-conducting tissue, surrounded by bulky frond bases, scales and abundant fibre.

Above: A tree fern may be up to 500 years old

In search of ferns

Fern-collecting was a popular hobby in the final thirty years of the reign of Queen Victoria and rainforests still existed close enough to Melbourne and Sydney for parties of fern-gatherers to make weekend picnic excursions. In Europe at the time, fern-collecting was said to make appreciable inroads into the abundance of ferns in the wild. In the twentieth century, magnificent ferns such as the Crows Nest shown above have often been taken from their natural habitat for garden display. Hopefully this practice is no longer followed.

Australia has only about 430 species of ferns, compared with more than 20,000 species of flowering plants.

Above: Crows Nest Fern growing on a tree stump

Take a closer look

To those who have never entered rainforest before, it may seem a threatening world. Travellers' tales about "the jungle" were traditionally full of rainforest nasties, which were outwitted with the aid of ancient tribal wisdom or by the narrator's own courageous action. An Australian rainforest is a milder place. There are a few precautions to note, however. If you meet a snake, admire it, then leave it strictly alone. Don't fiddle with the vegetation, especially plants with sharp hooks or with broad, furry stinging leaves. If you find yourself serving as mobile restaurant for a leech, a dob of Vegemite is a humane way to make it look elsewhere for a meal.

While coming to the realisation that the rainforest is not an unfriendly place, but is just going about its business, take a closer look at your surroundings. You will discover multitudinous miniature landscapes of wonder and delight.

Above: Detail of the moss-covered boulder opposite
Opposite: Boulder draped with moss and ferns, Daintree National Park, North Queensland

Fruits of the forest

The fruits of many rainforest trees and vines are borne high in the canopy. Their presence can be detected by the warblings, squawkings and flutterings of birds feeding upon them, letting discarded delicacies patter to the ground, where they lie in colourful disarray.

A fruit is a life-capsule dispatched by a tree to establish its descendants upon distant soil, since germination beneath the parent is an almost certain death-sentence for a seed. Rainforest fruits come in a variety of sizes and colours, designed to appeal to animals which will ingest the flesh and then void the seeds where they may have a chance of flourishing. Birds, bats and possums feast first at the canopy's table, while rats, mice, ground-dwelling birds and invertebrates dine at the second sitting, once the fruit has arrived on the ground.

Above: The Emerald Dove feeds on fruits on the rainforest floor
Opposite: Lillypilly fruits carpet the ground in Mount Glorious National Park, southeast Queensland

Targeting the consumer

A fruit's flesh serves as a bribe, offered to an animal in return for dispersing the fruit's seed far from the parent plant. The appearance of a fruit and the way in which it grows tells much about the sorts of animals which best suit this seed-dispersing objective. They will be attracted by the fruit's colour, will find the fruit convenient to pick and to eat, and will take no harm from chemical contents which repel or poison other animals less suitable for seed-dispersing purposes. Rainforest fruits need to defend themselves against the mechanical and chemical stresses of passing through an animal's digestive system. They may produce antibiotics and oils which protect them against bacteria or fungi.

Customers seeking fruit at the rainforest supermarket choose goods on their packaging, then eat the packaging and toss away the contents. Both producer and consumer are satisfied by the results of the transaction.

Above left and right: The fruits of the Atherton Oak and the Stinging Tree
Opposite, top left and clockwise: Pods and seeds of the Scarlet Bean; fruits of the Rusty or Port Jackson Fig; the capsules of the Pink Tamarind open to display glossy black seeds; the fruits of the Yellow Beech

The black seeds of the Topaz Tamarind are enclosed in red capsules

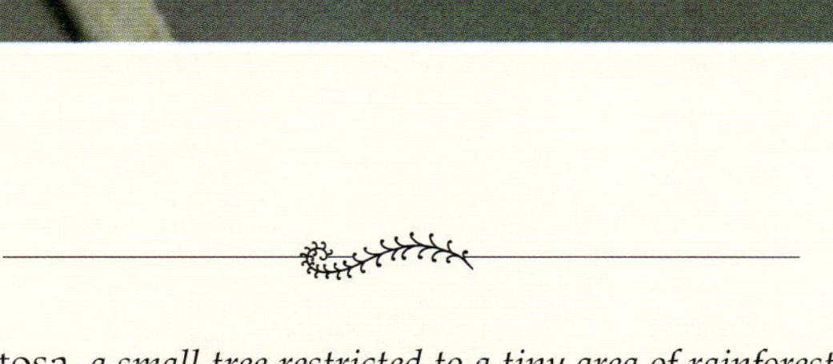

Fruits of Lethedon setosa*, a small tree restricted to a tiny area of rainforest in north Queensland*

Cassowary

A sword-blade of sunlight
thrusts through the palm-fans
to the forest floor beneath.
In a dazzle of light lie golden leaves,
blue fruit and a spinning-top fungus.
A helmeted giant blocks the light,
plucks the fruit, juggles and engulfs it.
The cassowary belies its martial image.
It is not a marauder,
but a benefactor,
sowing rainforest seed as it marches onwards.

Above: "... golden leaves, blue fruits
and a spinning-top fungus..."
Right: Cassowary habitat, Cape Tribulation, North Queensland

Giant in jeopardy

The giant, flightless Southern Cassowary, with its satiny black plumage, blue-pink neck and helmeted head, exists in several small, isolated populations in rainforests between Cape York and Townsville. The helmet acts as a shock-absorber as the cassowary runs, head lowered, through the forest. Where disturbance removes the trees upon whose fallen fruits the cassowary feeds, this remarkable bird soon vanishes. It is wary of humans unless diminishing habitat brings it into forced contact with them. The female is larger than the male, which incubates the eggs for around 30 days, then takes care of the chicks for at least four months.

Above: The Southern Cassowary eats large rainforest fruits and disperses their seeds

The indomitable fungi

Looking for fungi in the rainforest brings much reward for little effort, for these fascinating plants are everywhere. Moulds, yeasts and mildews are fungi. So are toadstools, mushrooms, puffballs and a myriad of sometimes exquisitely beautiful, sometimes grotesque organisms. Fungi possess no chlorophyll, so cannot use the sun's energy to manufacture food. Some exist as parasites on living creatures, while others obtain their energy from dead organic material. The easily-seen part of a fungus is the fruiting body, which contains spores. Less easily detected is the fine network of threads called hyphae which penetrates the food source, gathering nourishment. A fungus has no roots, no leaves and no flowers. Its spores are dispersed by wind or other means and each, after landing on a suitable situation, will grow into hyphae. No fruiting-body is produced until this network has united with hyphae from another spore of the same fungus species.

Above left and right: Bracket fungi grow in colonies, toadstools in dainty clusters, on tree trunks in Lamington National Park, Queensland

Opposite, top to bottom: Sunshine Fungus provides a patch of colour in the rainforest; Coral Fungus has delicate, branched upright arms; luminous fungus glows in dim light

Cup fungus

Overwhelmed by the immensity
of buttressed trees,
frustrated by the vain search
for creatures sensed but not seen,
I glance at a fallen log which bars the path.

I discover a miniature potter's bench,
littered with discards that the wheel
threw untrue,
with here and there
a terracotta masterpiece.

Above: Cup fungus growing on a fallen log

Givers, takers and partners

Rainforest fungi may be cup-shaped, shelf-shaped, bracket-shaped, phallus-shaped, basket-shaped, or take more traditional mushroom or puffball form. They are all fascinating. Many fungi feed upon dead plants or animals, helping return them to nature's cycle. Some fungi are parasites, taking nourishment from a plant or an animal without giving anything in return. A number of fungi live in relationships which benefit both partners. Some grow on the roots of living plants: the fungus feeds on excess carbohydrates from the other plant's surface roots and its partner takes in nutrients gathered by the fungus's vast network of hyphae (known as a mycelium). This partnership is believed to help plants growing in nutrient-poor soil.

Above: A fan-like bracket fungus

A festival of flowers

Gentle, pollen-carrying breezes are not common in rainforest and many rainforest plants depend on insects, birds or mammals such as bats to act as pollen couriers. The pollen-dispatching station, the flower, advertises by form, colour and/or scent that nectar is available. Red flowers are usually pollinated by birds, which have good colour vision. Pale or white flowers appeal to insects and may use scent as an additional lure for bats. Producing multitudes of flowers is a major energy investment. Rainforest trees may not flower until they are 30 to 40 years old, and then blossom only when conditions are right, perhaps every three or four years.

Top: The lime-green flowers of the Johnstone River Satinash
Above: The parasitic mistletoes draw nourishment from other plants
Opposite above: The flowers of the Fire-wheel Tree grow in brilliant clusters
Opposite below: Red flowers attract nectar-seeking birds

Top: The flowers on the trunk of this Bumpy Satinash are convenient for bats and other mammals to reach
Above: The exquisite flower cluster of Sayer's Silky Oak

Top: The Powderpuff Lillypilly is an understorey shrub of tropical rainforest
Above: The lovely Cooktown Orchid is the floral emblem of the State of Queensland

Cathedrals, rockets and treetrunks

It is said that the Gothic cathedrals of medieval times, with their high pinnacles and tall columns, were inspired by the towering forests of northern Europe. The architects of those cathedrals, faced with the problem of supporting a high, heavy roof on slender pillars, counterbalanced the outward thrust exerted by the roof with the inward thrust of ground-based stone flying buttresses. Six hundred years later, the problem of how to get a tall rocket to stand on its end before lift-off was solved by aeronautical engineers in the same fashion, by the use of metal tailfins.

Rainforest trees, which often grow on shallow soil, have been propping themselves in place with the aid of buttress roots for millions of years. These roots provide sheltered, humid habitats for all sorts of rainforest life - mosses, lichens, fungi, creepers and animals ranging from magnificent slugs to exquisitely-camouflaged geckos and fantastic insects.

Above left and right: Found on the buttress root shown opposite - Leaf-tailed Gecko and creeper
Opposite: Buttress root of rainforest tree, Daintree National Park, North Queensland

Frogs: an early-warning system

Frogs flourish in the humid rainforest, which is full of small, frog-friendly habitats. Rainforest frogs crouch on leaves, float in water-filled holes in treetrunks, swim in streams and lounge around in the leaf litter, eating insects and sometimes being eaten by snakes, lizards and other frogs. Most rainforest frogs produce eggs, which produce tadpoles, which become adult frogs. A few, like the Gastric-brooding Frog, whose eggs develop into froglets in the female's stomach, or the Marsupial Frog, whose male carries his young around in "hip-pocket" folds of skin, have their own unique ways of reproducing.

Frogs comprise an early-warning system for the rainforest. If the forest is healthy, frogs will be abundant. If frogs begin to disappear, examine the well-being of their forest home.

Above top left and clockwise: The normally pallid Pale Frog colours up when breeding; Fleay's Frog is disappearing from its SE Queensland/NE New South Wales rainforest habitat; the Red-eyed Tree-frog grasps branches with disc-tipped digits; the Nyakala Tree-frog was named after an Aboriginal tribe
Opposite above: Australia's tropical north houses a rich diversity of frog species. This is Daintree National Park
Opposite below: Green Tree-frogs mating. The male grasps the female under the armpits and sheds sperm over her eggs as they are laid

Discs on their fingers

Tree-frogs abound in the rainforest, clambering amongst the vegetation, leaping with long arms and legs outstretched to land spreadeagled on treetrunks and foliage. At rest, they tuck arms and legs beneath their bodies, half-close their eyes and blend into their surroundings. A tree-frog's fingers and toes end in discs which adhere to even the slickest surfaces. When it hunts at night, its magnificent eyes protrude like sports-car headlamps. A tree-frog's mouth bisects its head in a wide smile. Prey is zapped by a long, adhesive-tipped tongue, which flips the struggling insect, reptile or smaller frog back to be swallowed whole.

Above: This male Dainty Tree-frog is perched on a pandanus leaf, signalling his availability to a potential mate
Right: The Red-eyed Tree-frog is a nimble climber which descends to the ground to spawn in wet-season surface water

Top: The Cunjevoi Lily, with its sweet-scented flowers, grows in the understorey of the subtropical rainforest
Above: A Green Tree-frog waits the day away on a Cunjevoi leaf
Opposite: A Common Eggfly Butterfly rests for a moment on a Cunjevoi leaf

Following pages: A strangler fig envelops its host tree in Daintree National Park, North Queensland

Flyovers and freeways

In 1841, Clement Hodgkinson journeyed from the Hastings to the Bellingen Rivers. In *Australia from Port Macquarie to Moreton Bay*, he wrote of:

> "the countless species of creepers, wild vines and parasitical plants of singular conformation, which, interlaced and intertwined in inextricable confusion, bind and weave together the trees almost to their summits, and hang in rich and elegant flowering festoons from the highest branches."

Today, the splendid forests through which Hodgkinson travelled are sadly reduced. In the scattered stands which remain, creepers and vines still swing in elegant festoons, forming a network of aerial freeways and flyovers, along which scamper or crawl the myriad small lives of the forest.

Above: The Fawn-footed Melomys is an agile native rodent
Below: The Long-tailed Pygmy-possum has a prehensile tail
Left: Vine forest, Lamington National Park, southeast Queensland

Wake to the night

As the sun sets, many rainforest animals wake from sleep, groom themselves and move off to begin the night's activities.

Insectivorous bats lead the night-time parade, swooping from curled leaves, tree hollows and rocky crevices in the magic half-hour when evening becomes night. Many bats skim low over river or stream, scooping up the water, or lifting mouthfuls in their tail-membranes before bending to drink in flight. One species may even snatch tiny fish from the surface with the hooked claws of its slender legs. Some bats dash to and fro above the canopy, bouncing high-pitched tones from mouths or noses, picking up echoes from flying insects in huge leaflike ears, then scooping them from the air and crunching them noisily. A few species, such as the horseshoe-bats, may hang in ambush over forest paths like traffic policemen manning radar traps, using echolocation to detect oncoming insects.

Above: The sun setting over the Daintree River, North Queensland, is a cue for bats and other night creatures to waken
Opposite: The Diadem Horseshoe-bat lies in ambush, or patrols a rainforest flyway, taking passing insects from the air

Night-time is possum-time

After sunset, the rainforest becomes possum paradise. All possums are agile climbers, a number of species able to dangle from prehensile tails, while many can make amazing leaps between trees. Their relatives the gliders spread furry membranes between arms and legs as they volplane.

Cuscuses are found in Cape York's rainforests. They eat leaves, flowers and fruit, clambering through the trees, clutching branches with hands, feet and limber tails. The Striped Possum of North Queensland jumps boldly between trees, long tail streaming behind. It uses its elongated fourth finger and long tongue to retrieve wood-boring insect larvae. The rainforest-dwelling Coppery Brushtail Possum is closely related to the Common Brushtail of more southern forests. The fascinating Green Ringtail Possum sleeps on a lichen-encrusted branch, hunched into a furry ball, its "green" fur (the hairs are actually black, yellow and white) camouflaging it from predators.

Above: Spotted Cuscus
Opposite: Striped Possum

Following pages: left: Coppery Brushtail Possum; right: Green Ringtail Possum

Jurassic Park is alive and well

Under leaves, in fern-crowns, under slabs of rock and in cavities in massive treetrunks, the reptiles of the rainforest lurk and loiter, dreaming of the long ages when their forebears ruled the earth. From the tiniest almost-limbless skink slithering through the leaf-litter to the magnificent Green Python gift-wrapping a branch in shiny coils of emerald splendour, they have their own beauty. The few venomous snakes which live in Australian rainforests are shy and seldom-seen. Most rainforest reptiles are harmless to humans, though to the unwary tree-frog or luckless centipede a rainforest dragon or gecko may be as threatening as ever Velociraptor or Tyrannosaurus was to its long-ago prey.

Above: Southern Rainforest Dragon, northeastern New South Wales
Below: Chameleon Gecko, Mount Bartle Frere, North Queensland
Opposite: Green Python, Cape York, North Queensland

Following pages: Boyd's Rainforest Dragon, northeastern Queensland

A new national symbol

As the nineteenth century drew to a close, Australia's rainforest began to disappear, in fact and from public imagination. As nationalism grew, the symbol of Australia became the eucalypt, drought-adapted and able to cope with isolation in the settled landscape. The wide brown vista dotted with grey-green gums became the Australian image, so that when noted English artist Marianne North visited Australia she wrote of a spot that, "it was what Australians call 'a very pretty place', meaning that there was not a tree within a mile of it, and that it had a little water within reach."

As the twentieth century ends, the rainforests, with their abundance of trees and their spectacular waterfalls, are once again a focus of human attention. To this point, humans have taken advantage of the ancient forests. The time has come for the relationship to be transformed into one of harmony.

Preceding pages and above: Nandroya Falls, Wooroonooran National Park, North Queensland
Opposite: Millaa Millaa Falls, Atherton Tablelands, North Queensland

Following pages: Josephine Falls, Wooroonooran National Park, North Queensland

The arteries of the forest

Bounty of the sky, rain falls upon the forest canopy, plummeting from the drip-tips of countless leaves into the soil beneath. Some of the liquid is absorbed into hungry roots, while the remainder flows into creeks that chuckle over boulders and rapids, then thunder over waterfalls, to fill deep pools and source lowland-bound rivers. Freshwater turtles and the elusive Platypus are among the many creatures which make their home in the cool waters of rainforest streams.

Above: Eastern Long-necked Turtle
Below: Platypus in a rainforest stream
Left: Johnstone River, Wooroonooran National Park, North Queensland

Touch the forest and rejoice

The scents and sounds of the rainforest are often elusive and their sources high overhead. Vision may be baffled by the forest's dim light. Disregard all senses but touch, and run your hands over cool, waterworn rock. Plunge them into the cold, effervescent liquid which bubbles over mosaics of pebbles. Lichen-rough treetrunks, smooth fungi, delicate wisps of ferns, succulent mosses - all have their own delicious textures. And, if you can put aside natural prejudice, imagine stroking a sun-warm python, its smooth-scaled skin and powerful muscles a sensual joy beneath your fingertips.

Above: The rainforest offers multitudinous tactile delights
Opposite: Imagine touching a python, which is reaching out to touch you

All aboard and a safe voyage!

After heavy rainfall, as streams swirl through the rainforest they accumulate and sweep with them all the debris of the forest floor. Leaves and fruits, sticks and soil ride the tide, the heavier items sinking where the waterflow slows. Small creatures such as insects and spiders hitch rides on the flotsam.

Where trees are uprooted, or the forest disturbed, soil washes into the creeks and is carried downstream. Other, more harmful substances, such as pesticides and crop fertilisers, may also enter the forest from cultivation or clearing far upstream.

Above: Tropical rainforest creek at Cape Tribulation, North Queensland
Below: A damselfly floats downstream on a leaf
Left: Flotsam on a rainforest stream,
Cape Tribulation, North Queensland

Following pages: Cool temperate rainforest creek,
Melba Gully State Park, Otway Ranges, Victoria

There are crays in the creek

Rainforest creeks harbour hosts of whirligig beetles, caddis-fly larvae, giant waterbugs, water scorpions, dragonfly larvae, tadpoles, fish and the elusive Platypus. Smooth-shelled yabbies prowl warmer waters, while in fast-moving, colder mountain streams spiny freshwater crays are found. These colourful creatures may wander away from the water. If such an adventurer feels itself threatened, it will warn off the intruder with a loud hissing noise, produced by rubbing its "hand" against the side of its body armour.

Above: Euastacus *freshwater crayfish, Lamington National Park, southeastern Queensland*
Below: Tooloona Creek, Lamington National Park
Opposite: A stream in Lamington National Park is home to many aquatic creatures

Smaller disappears faster

The little furry animals of the rainforest have many traditional enemies, including meat-hungry quolls, constricting pythons, venomous snakes and soft-winged, sharp-taloned owls. For several thousand years, the Dingo has sneaked into the forest, snapping up anything it can catch. Today, traditional predators have been joined by those supreme hunters the fox and feral cat, and by the introduced and venomous Cane Toad, which has a voracious appetite and is death to most animals mouthing it. Secretive, timid and unobtrusive, small rainforest mammals may survive all these killers. However they cannot survive the wholesale destruction of their habitat.

Above: Brown Antechinus, a small marsupial common in rainforest, feeding on an insect
Right: Small-mammal habitat along creek banks, Tully Gorge National Park, North Queensland

Kingdoms built on sand

Some of the most unusual rainforests in the world grow on the sandmasses of Fraser Island and coastal Cooloola, in southeastern Queensland's Great Sandy Region. Here, the forest grows in sites protected from the ocean winds, some on sand dunes up to 260 metres in height. Here are rainforests, some with sclerophyll emergents, featuring Satinay and Brush Box trees, stately Kauri Pines and tall Piccabeen Palms, laced with vines and decorated with epiphytes. Sand contains little to nourish such forests: the minerals available for plant use are supplemented by wind-borne material. These sparse nutrients are utilised by the plants with the aid of networks of fungal hyphae. This recycling system works well until it is disrupted by clearing or fire, which opens the fragile topsoil to leaching by rain and dispersal by wind.

Above: The Wonga Pigeon is one of the birds found in the Great Sandy Region forests
Opposite: Wanggoolba Creek flows through rainforest on Fraser Island

The forest weeps

The forest is weeping
waterfalls of tears,
mourning its tall children
who fell before a ceasefire was declared.

Above: Erskine Falls, near Lorne, Victoria

The forest laughs

The forest laughs aloud in waterfalls,
giggles in delight in shimmering ripples
and chuckles quietly to itself
in the amorous croakings of frogs.

Above: Elabana Falls, Lamington National Park, southeastern Queensland

The water goes around and around

Until around three centuries ago, even those who thought deeply about the Earth and Nature believed that the fresh water found in rivers came from the centre of the earth. Towards the end of the seventeenth century, Edmund Halley (of Halley's Comet fame) calculated that the amount of water falling as snow and rain on southern Europe and North Africa roughly equalled the water flowing from rivers into the Mediterranean Sea. He was the first scientist to grasp the process by which water circulates from earth to sky and back to earth once again and he eventually worked out the cycle of monsoon rains which waters the tropical and subtropical rainforests of the world.

Above left: Hopetoun Falls, Otway Ranges, Victoria
Above right: Beauchamp Falls, Otway Ranges, Victoria
Opposite: Russell Falls, Mount Field National Park, Tasmania

Following pages: Chalahn Falls, Lamington National Park, southeastern Queensland

At the edge

The eucalypt-dominated dry sclerophyll forest known generally as "bushland" typical of much of Australia replaced the rainforests during the millions of years after separation from Antarctica. While the crowns of rainforest trees fit together like pieces of a jigsaw, in dry sclerophyll forest each crown stands in its own space. Rainforest trees have leaves which transpire water readily and whose drip-tips shed rain, while the leaves of dry sclerophyll plants are leathery, waxy or hairy, reduced, or have become spikes, to lessen transpiration during drought. The frontline between rainforest and dry sclerophyll is not always clear, and some rainforests include tall emergent trees such as Rose Gum, Brush Box and Ash.

Above: Where rainforest meets bushland
Opposite: Laughing Kookaburras, birds of the bushland, venture into rainforest

Some are adaptable

In Victoria, cool temperate rainforest is now found only in isolated pockets in the Otway Ranges, the Central Highlands, the Strzelecki Ranges, on Wilsons Promontory and in East Gippsland. This splendid forest has been cleared or logged extensively and the total remaining area is less than 13 000 hectares. The extent of change in such forests may be masked from the casual eye by the persistence of eye-catching plants such as tree-ferns, which prefer wet forests, but may adapt to the forest edges and even to cleared areas if their roots can stand in wet soil. There are adaptable animal species as well, which manage to survive even if the forests disappear or become altered to bushland, so long as there remains food to eat and some measure of shelter.

Above: The Diamond Python lives in a variety of arboreal habitats
Below: The Lowland Copperhead lives near water in a variety of ecological niches
Right: Tarra-Bulga National Park, Strzelecki Ranges, Victoria

Where rainforest meets reef

The rainforest and the Great Barrier Reef are two of Australia's best-known attractions and together form a focus for domestic and international tourism. Some once-isolated areas of splendid rainforests, such as the stretch between the Daintree River and Cape Tribulation, are proving prime targets for residential development. Many people want to live in or near rainforest and reef. They also want modern conveniences and comforts and easy access to their homes. Few pause to think that, carved up by roads, golf courses, shopping centres and hobby farms, the rainforest they admire so much will be degraded to less than its former splendour.

There is an old saying that if you truly love a living thing you do not seek to possess it, for clutching it to you will, in the end, destroy it and leave you grieving. Perhaps those who would love the rainforest to its ultimate disadvantage should take heed.

Above: Buff-breasted Paradise Kingfisher
Left: Cape Tribulation, North Queensland

Above: The larvae of the Cairns Birdwing Butterfly feed on the leaves of one species of rainforest vine

Above: Pied Imperial-Pigeons nest on offshore Reef islands, flying to the mainland rainforest each day to feed

A world heritage

In 1873, George Elphinstone Dalrymple journeyed by whale boat up a North Queensland river and later wrote that, "no river-reach in North Australia possesses surroundings combining so much of distant mountain grandeur with local beauty and wealth of vegetation." He commented on the enormous quantities of Red Cedar growing along the river, which he named the Daintree, after a geologist friend who was Agent General for Queensland. Soon timber-cutters arrived, and within ten years the cedar had been logged out. Cattle and sugarcane farming were later established on the cleared land.

Today, the Daintree National Park extends from the Bloomfield River in the north to the Mossman River in the south. The entire area from Cooktown south to Paluma was given World Heritage Listing in 1988, for its fauna and flora of outstanding universal value and its natural beauty.

Above: Rainforest, Daintree National Park, North Queensland
Opposite: Rapids in the Mossman River, Daintree National Park

Strutting the branches

The ground-dwelling kangaroos familiar to all of us cannot move their hindfeet independently unless they are swimming.

The remarkable tree-kangaroos grip branches with the strong claws of their forefeet and walk forwards or backwards with alternate movements of their short, broad hindfeet. Descending a tree, a tree-kangaroo moves its forefeet alternately down the trunk, while sliding on its clasped hindfeet. It may leap from one tree to another, or jump to the ground from as high as 15 metres. On the ground, a tree-kangaroo hops, with its tail held in the air.

Above: The granular soles of this Lumholtz's Tree-kangaroo form non-skid surfaces
Left: Tree-kangaroo habitat, Daintree National Park, North Queensland

Dependent on the forests

Flying-foxes' scientific name, *Pteropus*, means "wing-footed", and the fingers of a flying-fox's hand are joined by delicate yet strong, crepey skin, which stretches to drumhead tautness as the owner takes flight. Flying-foxes are night-time foragers, which eat fruits, nectar and pollen. The forest serves as their food supply, their place of refuge and the nursery for their young. Those people who enjoy contemplating Nature's puzzles should have a particular interest in flying-foxes. They are conventionally grouped with the smaller insectivorous bats, but their eyes are "wired" to their brains in a fashion similar to that found in primates and quite unlike that found in the smaller, insect-eating "microbats". More than 20 other features peculiar to primates apply to flying-foxes and some experts argue that they are more closely related to lemurs, apes and humans than to the microbats.

Above: The large eyes of the Grey-headed Flying-fox denote its nocturnal nature
Opposite: This Spectacled Flying-fox is about to launch itself in flight

Song-Star of the forest

In 1865, in his *Handbook to the Birds of Australia*, John Gould wrote of the Superb Lyrebird as follows: "Were I requested to suggest an emblem for Australia among its avifauna, I should without the slightest hesitation select the Lyre-bird as the most appropriate." He also noted that, "At Illawarra it is sometimes pursued by dogs trained to rush suddenly upon it, when it immediately leaps upon the branch of a tree, and, its attention being attracted by the dog which stands barking below, it is more easily approached and shot."

Why shoot a lyrebird? In 1865, to supply filmy plumes to be used as decorations for fashionable women's hats. Today, the Superb Lyrebird survives in southeastern Australia where corridors for the dispersal of young birds still exist between adjoining forests. It has been introduced into two localities in Tasmania.

Above: Male Superb Lyrebird
Opposite: The Superb Lyrebird has been introduced to the Mount Field and Hastings areas in Tasmania

Who's viewed a potoroo?

A number of small marsupials are popularly lumped together as "rat-kangaroos". They are the Musky Rat-kangaroo, the bettongs and the potoroos. For survival these animals need dense ground cover, and they disappear where this is destroyed by fire, or by clearing for agriculture. The introduction of the fox, which preys efficiently upon small mammals, has hastened their decline. Only two of the nine known species of potoroo-like animals are often seen today, and even these are becoming less common.

The hare-sized potoroos look like small, compact wallabies and have short but well-muscled forelegs, which are used to dig for underground fungi, roots, grubs and spiders. Their tails are capable of gripping objects and are used to carry nesting material. The Long-nosed Potoroo was one of the first mammals recorded from Australia (Captain Arthur Phillip described it in 1789). Today, it may be seen in wet coastal forests from southeastern Queensland to western Victoria. It rarely ventures far from the protection of dense undergrowth but a quiet, careful watcher may spot it feeding after dusk. The Long-footed Potoroo was described as a new species in 1980. It has been found only in two tiny areas of high-rainfall forest in eastern Gippsland, Victoria.

Above: The Long-nosed Potoroo lives in coastal wet forests from southeastern Queensland to western Victoria
Left: Victoria's high-rainfall forest is the habitat of the Long-footed Potoroo

Death in the forest

The tiny lives of the rainforest - minute worms, molluscs, spiders and insects, which live in the leaf-litter, under bark and amongst the burgeoning plants - are eagerly eaten by larger invertebrates. These armoured predators are themselves prey for lizards, frogs, snakes and small carnivorous marsupials. At the top of the foodchain are the great predators, the owls, which specialise in possums and gliders, the quolls, which favour small marsupials, reptiles and insects, the large pythons, which can dispose of pademelons, small wallabies and possums and that opportunistic rover the Dingo, which will eat anything large enough to make a mouthful and slow enough to catch. Just as rainforest plants have to survive in a world of intense competition, rainforest animals must remain wary and utilise every defensive tactic if they are not to end up in the body-count of some keen-eyed hunter.

Above: The Dingo may hunt in rainforest, preying upon ground animals
Opposite: The Masked Owl takes gliders, bandicoots and other mammals, as well as roosting birds

" ... the birds approach gently ..."

The majority of Europeans who entered rainforest in the nineteenth century thought of it as hostile, to be conquered with axe and fire. There were, however, wiser souls, who realised that the forest's greatest rewards are reserved for the wooer rather than for the rapist. Carl Lumholtz, the anthropologist and zoologist whose explorations of the rainforest were facilitated by his willingness to learn from the Aborigines, wrote:

> "On first entering the scrub, the solemn quiet and solitude which reign are striking. You work your way through it by the sweat of your brow; you startle a bird, which at once disappears, and your prevailing impression is that there is no life. But if you come there in the early morning or towards evening, and sit down quietly, it is surprising to see the birds approach gently, as if they had been called, and disappearing as noiselessly as they came."

Above: Eastern Yellow Robin nesting in rainforest
Left: The rainforest in Lamington National Park, southeastern Queensland is world-famous for its birdlife

The pollinators

Australia's rainforest trees may be pollinated by bats or by butterflies, bees or other insects. Many are pollinated by birds, especially by lorikeets and honeyeaters, whose brush-tipped tongues allow them to delve deeply into flowers' stores of nectar, emerging gold-headed with pollen-grains to be carried onwards.

After a tree species is eliminated from a rainforest, the animals which pollinated it may disappear. Where pollinating animals decline in numbers, trees upon whose nectar or flowers they fed will fail to set seed.

Above: Lewin's Honeyeater belongs to a nectar-seeking, flower-pollinating group of Australian birds
Opposite: Rainforest, Mount Warning National Park, northeastern New South Wales

Following pages: Subtropical rainforest

Above top to bottom: Birds of the rainforest and its verges: Spectacled Flycatcher; Grey Fantail; Grey-headed Robin
Opposite: Male Lovely Wren feeding chick

A bountiful harvest

For many centuries, every few years when the Bunya Pines of southeast Queensland fruited, Aborigines gathered from hundreds of kilometres around to gather the cones. "They valued the trees very highly, for they would have killed anyone who had cut one down to get the cones, tho' the trees were very prickly and unpleasant to climb", wrote a white observer. (Women had the unenviable job of climbing the trees to retrieve the fruit.) Today, the forest which remains on the Bunya Mountains is still a dark and magical place, a paradise for birdwatchers, where the cries of bowerbirds and parrots echo the excited voices of long-ago tribal groups gathering in peace for the Bunya-nut harvest.

Above: Bunya Pine
Opposite: Female Satin Bowerbird on a Bunya Pine branch

The bower-builders

Mature male bowerbirds construct and maintain playgrounds or bowers, around which they place "treasures" appropriate to their species. They sing and dance with their treasures in order to attract duller-plumaged females, who are mated in or near the bowers, then go off to build nests and rear young with no help from the males. Young, female-plumaged males may visit bowers, apparently learning construction skills.

The Golden Bowerbird, which builds a "maypole" bower decorated with lichens and mosses, lives exclusively in rainforest at altitudes between 650 and 1900 metres in a small area of northeastern Queensland. The Regent Bowerbird of coastal southeastern Queensland and northeastern New South Wales rainforest is nowhere abundant. One population of Satin Bowerbirds lives in rainforest above 600 metres in the Atherton region of northeastern Queensland, another in lowland, more southerly coastal areas. The male Satin Bowerbird may paint his bower with vegetable substances and his treasury contains blue objects and flowers.

Above left: Male Regent Bowerbird in his bower
Above right: Male Golden Bowerbird
Opposite: Male Satin Bowerbird constructing a bower

" ... like living jets of crimson flame"

In 1868, the poet Henry Kendall celebrated the rainforest as follows:

"All day long these deep, grand solitudes are ringing with the varied voices of their innumerable feathered denizens:- ...satin birds (bowerbirds) throwing abroad their singular cries from the meshes of a semi-tropical jungle ...gorgeous parrots among the taller saplings, leaping from bough to bough like living jets of crimson flame; magnificent 'regent birds' and 'riflemen' standing from their leafy cover, gloriously decked in full splendour of their unrivalled plumage; and millions of nameless twittering things flashing to and fro 'like shattered meteors' all combined, animate these Eden-like scenes from year to year."

Above left: Male Eclectus Parrot
Above right: Female Eclectus Parrot
Opposite: Rainbow Lorikeets on Umbrella Tree

Following pages: Male Australian King-Parrot

Life on the ground floor

Near the rainforest floor, the air is still, the humidity high and the light often dim. Some types of rainforests, with more open canopies, have a tangled understorey of herbs, ferns and saplings. In others, only very shade-tolerant plants and fungi survive amongst the buttress roots of the trees. A variety of animals finds food in the litter on the forest floor, while the male Australian Brush-Turkey makes use of plant debris to build an incubator for eggs.

Above: The understorey of some rainforests is sparse
Below: The male Australian Brush-Turkey scratches plant debris into a large incubator mound
Left: On the floor of the forest

Top: The Red-legged Pademelon eats the fallen leaves and fruits of rainforest trees
Above: The tiny Musky Rat-kangaroo lives only in northern Queensland rainforests, where it feeds in the leaf litter on invertebrates and fallen fruits. It carries nesting material with its tail

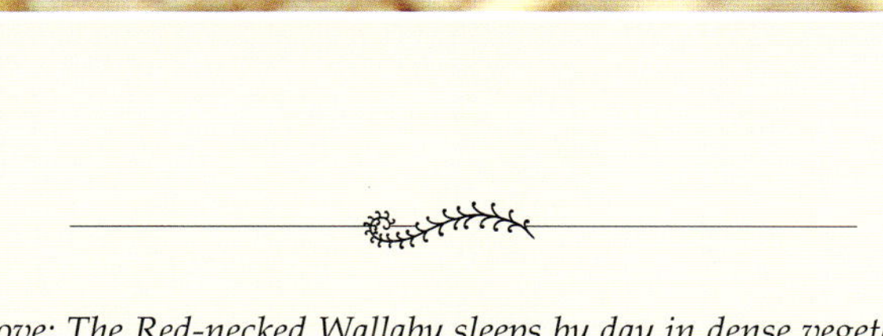

Above: The Red-necked Wallaby sleeps by day in dense vegetation and moves to the forest verges at night to feed

Above, top to bottom: Bandy-bandy; Brown Tree-snake; Eastern Tiger Snake

Top and above: Eastern Water-dragon; Brown-striped Frog

The Aboriginal people and the rainforest

Europeans have been interacting with Australia's rainforests for just over 200 years. When Europeans arrived, Aboriginal people had lived in parts of the continent for at least 50,000 years. During that time, rainforest was one of the many habitats used by various groups as a food-source, though probably only in northern Queensland was there enough rainforest to support a permanent human population.

Carl Lumholtz reported in 1889 that these rainforest-dwelling Aborigines built waterproof huts, used flat stone axes and captured prey in pits, nets and traps of vine or fibre.

Many of their vegetable foods required sophisticated preparation to remove toxic elements.

Some rainforest sites are associated with Aboriginal traditional stories and have long been places of spiritual significance to the Aborigines of the area.

Many Aboriginal groups utilised fire to drive game, promote vegetation growth and to clear ground cover. It is possible that some rainforest stands may have been protected by burning fire-breaks around them, which may also have inhibited their expansion.

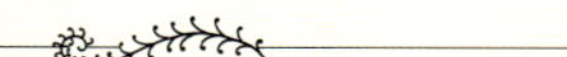

Above left and right: Nargun's Den, in Mitchell River National Park, Victoria, had special significance for the Aborigines of the area

Rainforest revelation

From today's sunscorched plain,
we zigzag up the time-tunnel mountain road
into a forest from the past,
where trees wear cloaks of moss,
ruffles of lacy ferns and plumes of orchids.

A step beneath the canopy,
and brilliant wings bless us in their passing,
invite us to wander
along cool pathways to still pools,
sit in silence and listen to the leaves talking overhead.

Astonished by joy,
we find in our hearts
answers
to questions we did not know we needed to ask.

Above: In the rainforest
Right: Palm frond

" These rainforests reach their most abundant lushness in north Queensland, in particular on the so-called Atherton-Herberton Tableland, where one single uninterrupted belt of genuine tropical nature covers the basalt plateau. ..... This was virgin rainforest and the white man's axe had not yet started its destruction."

ERIC MJÖBERG
Amongst Stone Age People in the Queensland Wilderness
(translated by S.M. Fryer)

Mjöberg's expedition to Queensland started from Stockholm in 1912 and he appears to have visited the Atherton Tableland in February 1913. The account of the Tableland above is dated April 1918. The years since have wrought tremendous changes to the Tableland, as the photograph above shows.

The rainforests of Australia

Dr Aila Keto AO

The earliest and most vivid childhood memory I have of rainforest is biting into a Davidson's Plum, much like a dark, oversized muscatel grape with its beautiful bluish bloom promising delicious juices and a delectable feast. It was not palatable at all, extremely tart in fact, but I loved the mystery of the bush and its forbidden fruits. I remember El Arish where I grew up as the most wondrous place on earth, a meeting place of two worlds - one, a myriad of coral reefs and islands where dolphins and whales swam in waters sometimes so mirror-smooth they reflected the islands and the clouds, where seabirds nested so densely it was impossible to walk amongst them; the other, the rainforests with babbling creeks and waterfalls and a never-ending profusion of plants, birds, butterflies and other stunning creatures. The Cassowary, with its huge black glistening body, large dark eyes, blue neck and crimson wattle, was its proud and potent symbol.

Today, my old reef haunts are dead and crumbled. The rainforest is cleared. Even the creek I played and swam in has vanished, silted up and filled in completely. The saddest thing is that all of us can tell such tragic tales. Each loss adds up over the years to why three-quarters of all our rainforests have gone in the 200 years after Europeans first arrived.

The same is happening worldwide. Already, half the world's rainforests have been destroyed. Every minute we spend looking at the wonderful images in this book, an area of rainforest the size of a football field is being felled. In another 50 years the world's rainforests will have all but disappeared and with them more than half the species of plants and animals on Earth. Such a loss is unimaginable.

You could say we don't need to worry in Australia. Our rainforests, less than 0.3 per cent of the world's total, seem so insignificant beside those of the mighty Amazon, New Guinea or Zaire. We couldn't be more wrong. Australia's rainforests contain the greatest concentrations of relict and primitive biota anywhere on Earth.

These ancient elements miraculously survived because Australia escaped the brunt of a massive asteroid collision 65 million years ago. The ensuing impact-winter largely wiped out the ancient rainforests of the Northern Hemisphere. Then from 40 million years ago whilst the rest of the world cooled, Australia, through a freak and fortunate coincidence, moved northward towards equatorial warmth thus keeping conditions constant enough to preserve its ancient stocks. These stocks in Australia even survived the last Ice Ages that saw Europe and North America under massive ice sheets hundreds of metres thick.

Opposite: Rainforests have been cleared to make space for agriculture and grazing
Below: The gastric-brooding frogs are typical of rainforest species which have contributed to human welfare. They are disappearing and may already be gone forever

Our climate has since collapsed almost entirely. Australia today is the most arid and infertile continent on earth. It is a miracle rainforests have survived at all. Their closed canopies protect a fragile microclimate out of phase with the outside by thousands of years. Destroy this microclimate and you risk the forest's very survival.

Despite being fragile, fragmented and only a fraction of their former glory, they are part of what makes Australia unique. They are living museums of ancestral rainforests that once stretched from Greenland to Patagonia. They are the birthplace of a myriad of flora and fauna uniquely adapted to our harsh, dry island continent. In the 7000 kilometres of coastline from Broome to Tasmania, from the mountains to the sea, we retain the most diverse assemblage of rainforest patches over the greatest stretch of terrain of any country on Earth. Tropical, subtropical and temperate rainforests form the three core elements of our rainforest heritage.

Above: Clearing of rainforest at Cape Tribulation

TROPICAL RAINFORESTS, the oldest and botanically most diverse, have their major last bastion in Queensland where more than half Australia's rainforests survive. The largest single area, 750 000 hectares in total, occurs in the Wet Tropics of Queensland World Heritage Area. The highest concentration of primitive flowering plant families in the world finds refuge there. Only one-thousandth of the area of Australia, it is home to more than 3000 plant species, a third of the continent's mammal species, half of the bird species and one-quarter of the frogs and reptiles. At least 700 plant species and 70 of the vertebrate animals are found nowhere else. Eighty-six plants and animals are now on the verge of extinction. The major threats come from past and ongoing clearing, weeds, feral animals and disruption of habitat by a myriad of criss-crossed access roads and old logging tracks. The largely pristine rainforests in the McIlwraith and Iron Ranges of Cape York have fared better and stand a good chance of surviving intact. In the monsoon tropics of northern Australia, rainforests now survive only in small, sufficiently wet, fire-proof and isolated patches and are highly vulnerable to extinction from fire, weeds, feral animals and grazing. The Northern Territory's Arnhem Land has at least 204 000 hectares in thousands of small patches associated with sandstone gorges, seepage zones or springs. The Kimberley region of Western Australia, one of the last great wilderness areas of the world, has more than fifteen hundred small relict patches totalling about 7000 hectares.

SUBTROPICAL RAINFORESTS, simpler in structure and diversity, dominated much of the world 55 to 40 million years ago. Their present-day survivors have been mostly cleared everywhere. Nutrient-rich lowlands and gentler tablelands were hardest hit. Fragmented remnants are all that remain. Many may be too small to survive in the longer term. Queensland and northern New South Wales are probably their last stronghold in the world. As fragmented islands in a sea of hostile environments, invaded by weeds and frequent fires, their future in a warming Greenhouse world looks uncertain. Less than 10 per cent of Queensland's subtropical rainforests are protected in National Parks. They still survive mainly between Eungella west of Mackay and the Richmond-Tweed district in northern New South Wales.

More than 90 per cent of New South Wales' rainforests grow in the State's northeast. Only about a third have been included in the World Heritage List. These rainforests extending into southern Queensland represent a remarkable assembly of ancient flowering plants, many rare and threatened, and the closest living relatives of ancestral temperate rainforests. Any with eucalypts amongst them are now being logged.

TEMPERATE RAINFORESTS had their heyday 36 to 25 million years ago. The cool temperate forms at high altitudes and latitudes are the least complex botanically but grandiose and cathedral-like. Often only one or two tree species dominate. They are rare world-wide and highly threatened by Greenhouse warming. Tasmania, with about one-third of Australia's rainforests, is one of the world's last strongholds. Whilst significant stands are in the World Heritage area, the majority in the magnificent Tarkine area to the northwest are unprotected. King Billy Pine, a long-lived relative of the Californian Redwood, does not return after fire.

In Victoria, no more than 16 000 hectares of eucalypt-free temperate rainforests remain, in the Otway and Strzelecki Ranges, the Central Highlands and East Gippsland. The largest single patch of cool temperate rainforest is no more than 150 hectares. Small patches of warm temperate rainforest survive only in East Gippsland's coastal lowlands.

More widespread, both in Victoria and Tasmania, and equally important are the beautiful rainforests with tall eucalypts rising majestically above the canopies. These tragically are prime targets for logging, both for woodchips and sawn timbers.

THE FUTURE OF AUSTRALIA'S RAINFORESTS depends on us. They are like fragile living organisms, expanding and contracting over the millennia in response to climate change and the ravages of fire. Only when we see them as a living dynamic landscape will we be able to save them. They have retracted from covering almost the entire continent 50 million years ago to less than 0.3 per cent of the continent today. When habitat losses reach 90 per cent, half the species will go forever - if not now, then some time in the future. Their die is cast. Many of the isolated patches will not survive the combined pressures of natural catastrophes or fire, weeds, pests, and future climate change. Many populations are already on their way to becoming extinct.

To avert disaster we must try, in the next 200 years, to reverse the damage of the past 200 - not just repair and protect what is left but restore as much as we can of what has been lost. That is why Project Gondwana was born - to identify, protect and restore our irreplaceable Gondwanan heritage.

Every fragment of rainforest in the patchwork must form a core on which to build, forming a network of Great Australian Rainforest Parks. Edges can be expanded and new patches planted to restore the links - all according to a national plan, a plan which also brings endangered species back from the brink.

That is the challenge - for governments, scientists and the people of Australia.

THERE IS HOPE for our rainforests. Alone, we might find the task of saving the remaining forests and restoring those we have destroyed as daunting. Together, generation by generation we can achieve miracles. But time is running out.

Dr Aila Keto AO, is a biochemist, who is founder and President of the Australian Rainforest Conservation Society. In 1992, she received the Fred M Packard International Parks Merit Award for her dedication to rainforest preservation. Her other awards include Avon 'Spirit of Achievement' Award (1993), BHP Bicentennial Award 1988, UNEP Global 500 Roll of Honour 1988, Advance Australia Foundation Award 1988. In 1994 she was made an Officer of the Order of Australia.

Western Australian rainforests are confined to small patches of up to three hectares of vegetation in wet gullies and are too small to be shown in the map above.

"WHAT CAN I DO TO HELP PRESERVE AND RESTORE RAINFORESTS?"

Australian rainforests, where so many elements of ancient Gondwana have miraculously survived, are today facing an extinction crisis, largely at our hands. We will lose an irreplaceable heritage unless we as a nation care enough and act. Project Gondwana was born out of this critical need to identify, protect and restore that heritage. All types of rainforest, especially those that include eucalypts, are variously threatened. Their future is in our hands.

THE AUSTRALIAN RAINFOREST CONSERVATION SOCIETY HAS:

- Led the campaign that stopped logging in the rainforests of North Queensland and prepared the nomination that gained their World Heritage Listing.
- Compiled and presented scientific arguments to the Commission of Inquiry that brought an end to logging on Fraser Island; prepared the case that led to its World Heritage Listing.
- Successfully campaigned against rainforest logging on the Central Queensland coast, thus ending, in 1994, all logging of "pure" rainforest in the State.

Now, the Society needs to grow to match the scale of the problem Australia-wide.

YOU CAN HELP STOP THE LOSS OF OUR RAINFORESTS!

- Join the Australian Rainforest Conservation Society. Become part of Project Gondwana.
- Write to the Prime Minister urging his active support for the "Great Australian Rainforest Parks" concept with adequate funding for acquisition and management.
- Write to the Premier of your State asking that all remaining areas of rainforest be placed in large, viable conservation reserves.
- Avoid using rainforest timbers for building or furniture.
- Visit a rainforest to reinvigorate your passion for saving them.
- Join the "Back from the Brink" project in which you adopt a threatened rainforest animal or plant, learn more and raise funds for its survival plan.
- Become part of "Rainforests 2200", a 200-year national plan to restore lost and damaged rainforests.
- Donate generously to the Australian Rainforest Conservation Society.

TOGETHER WE CAN MAKE A DIFFERENCE

For further information: The Australian Rainforest Conservation Society
19 Colorado Avenue
Bardon Queensland 4065 Australia
Telephone (07) 3368 1318
Facsimile (07) 3368 3938

Membership fees: $20 single; $30 joint/family; $10 concession

WHEN YOU JOIN THE SOCIETY, YOU WILL RECEIVE:

- A 16-page booklet of information about Australian rainforests, with suggestions for school projects, student activities, and hands-on programs to help protect and restore rainforests
- A car-sticker bearing the Australian Rainforest Conservation Society frog logo
- A pack of six superb rainforest postcards

Copies of the Rainforest Information Booklet can be obtained separately from the above address at a nominal cost of $5.00 which includes postage and handling.

Acknowledgements

Dr John Winter introduced Steve to rainforest and opened his eyes to the wonders of forest wildlife, particularly possums. For that we will be eternally grateful.

Don Burrows' flute echoed through the rainforest over fifteen years ago and awakened in Steve the poetry of rainforest. That poetry still remains.

Ian Morris has recently planted "botanical seeds" in Steve's imagination. (Jan's love of all things green has been with her since childhood.) Ian has also contributed some hard-to-find "creature-photos" for this book.

While Steve and Stan Breeden have almost crossed paths many times over the three decades they have spent photographing Australia, it has only been recently that they have teamed up on publishing projects. We greatly appreciate use of many of Stan's outstanding plant and wildlife photographs for this book.

Pat Slater has crafted a manuscript that brings our vision to life. Pat's energy, enthusiasm and dedication are a constant source of inspiration.

Raoul Slater provided photographs of bowerbirds and an Eastern Yellow Robin and Peter Slater provided a delightful shot of an Emerald Dove. Pip McConnel provided the design, Greg Sullivan scanned the images and Matt Naughton print-produced. We thank you all.

We particularly thank Dr Aila Keto and Dr Keith Scott of the Australian Rainforest Conservation Society, for providing a technical review and information, and for writing our section on rainforest conservation. Aila and Keith's untiring efforts have contributed greatly to rainforest conservation and for that we sincerely thank you both.

Finally, we thank Peter Stanton whose life-long commitment to conservation has greatly inspired Steve.

Steve and Jan Parish

PRODUCTION DETAILS
Photography - Steve Parish
Additional photography - Stanley Breeden, Ian Morris, Raoul Slater, Peter Slater
Photographic editing - Jan Parish and Steve Parish
Text, poetry and editing - Pat Slater, Steve Parish Publishing
Text on conservation - Dr Aila Keto, Australian Rainforest Conservation Society
Design and artwork - Pip McConnel, Steve Parish Publishing
Cover design - Paul Byrne, Steve Parish Publishing **Artwork** - Robyn Russell
Colour separations - Greg Sullivan, Steve Parish Publishing
Print production - Matt Naughton, Steve Parish Publishing
Printed in Australia - Inprint Limited **Binding** - Podlich Enterprises

First published in Australia by Steve Parish Publishing Pty Ltd
PO Box 2160 Fortitude Valley BC Queensland 4006

National Library of Australia cataloguing in publication data:
Parish, Steve. Parish, Jan - Australian Rainforest
ISBN 0947263 83 7
1. Photography - Australia
2. Title - Australian Rainforest